Praise for the Dating Goddess

The *Adventures in Delicious Dating After 40* series of books is based on the blog Adventures in Delicious Dating After 40 at www.DatingGoddess.com. Here are comments from readers.

♥ "Adventures in Delicious Dating After 40 is a wonderful composite of both the mechanics of post-40 online dating and what the practice of honoring one's self actually looks like. How marvelous your writing is to read. I spent about 2 hours reading and was riveted the whole time." —Maggie Hanna

♥ "At last, a dating writer who addresses requirements. You are SO right on! I'm thrilled to have found you!" —Rachel Sarah, author, *Single Mom Seeking*

♥ "Powerfully heartfelt and honest writing. You are inspiring." —Kare Anderson, Emmy Award winning writer

"I just love your writing. It is very fresh and gives the reader something to think about." —Kelly Lantz, President & Manager, 55-Alive.com

"Dating Goddess, you are like a, a, a, well, a goddess to me. You've helped guide me successfully through my re-entry into the dating world after 14 years. I'm an eager student and fast study, and do get myself into situations that others don't know how to deal with — such as 3 dates in one day -— so thankfully you are there! You're the greatest, thanks for all you do for us!" —Jae G.

"I find your point of view much more interesting than other dating writers. Thanks for always reminding me to enjoy dating life no matter what it throws at you." —Sandy

"I love Adventures in Delicious Dating After 40. I really do like your honest and authentic voice — it's refreshing." —Wendy S.

"Adventures in Delicious Dating After 40 is really fun to read. Thanks for sharing your thoughts and letting us divorced single women know that we are not alone. There's a lot here that I identify with, although I'm not as brave as you are about dating lots of guys. So far. Love your blog — the first blog I've ever read consistently." —Elizabeth

"Thanks for a wonderful blog. You're doing a great job of saying what's in my mind. There's rarely a day I miss when it comes to checking in on your wisdom." —Paulette Ensign

Check Him Out *Before* Going Out

Avoiding Dud Dates

by **Dating Goddess**

Check Him Out Before Going Out: Avoiding Dud Dates

Second Edition

Cover design by Dave Innis, www.innisanimation.com

Book design by JustYourType.biz

Printed in the United States of America.

ISBN   Print: 978-1-930039-38-4

        eBook   978-1-930039-16-2

How to order:

The *Adventures in Delicious Daing After 40* books may be ordered directly from www.DatingGoddess.com.

Quantity discounts are also available. Visit us online for updates and additional articles.

The Adventures in Delicious Dating After 40 books are dedicated to my ex-husband since he unexpectedly released me to explore the untethered life of a single woman. I then had the freedom for the experiences, lessons and insights shared in these pages.

Books by Dating Goddess

- *Date or Wait: Are You Ready for Mr. Great?*

- *Assessing Your Assets: Why You're A Great Catch*

- *In Search of King Charming: Who Do I Want to Share My Throne?*

- *Embracing Midlife Men: Insights Into Curious Behaviors*

- *Dipping Your Toe in the Dating Pool: Dive In Without Belly Flopping*

- *Winning at the Online Dating Game: Stack the Deck in Your Favor*

- *Check Him Out Before Going Out: Avoiding Dud Dates*

- *First-Rate First Dates: Increasing the Chances of a Second Date*

- *Real Deal or Faux Beau: Should You Keep Seeing Him?*

- *Multidating Responsibly: Play the Field Without Being A Player*

- *Moving On Gracefully: Break Up Without Heartache*

- *From Fear to Frolic: Get Naked Without Getting Embarrassed*

- *Ironing Out Dating Wrinkles: Work Through Challenges Without Getting Steamed*

Contents

X

Introduction

This book is designed for anyone who is interested in stories, advice, and lessons from the midlife dating front. If you are over 40 and haven't dated in a while — or even if you have — you'll learn ways to approach dating with zeal, optimism, and hope. Even if you've had more than your share of negative experiences, I'll share how to glean lessons from those adventures, rather than just declaring that "all men are jerks" or "men are just looking for sex."

While most of the perspective is from a woman to women, men's comments, experiences, and lessons have been integrated as appropriate.

This book began as daily entries into my blog, Adventures in Delicious Dating After 40, which has been featured in the *Wall Street Journal* as well as on radio and TV. I wrote about my epiphanies from my and my friends' dating life. The best postings were culled to make this and subsequent books.

This book focuses on what you need to ask before agreeing to even a coffee date. You need to vet the men who email and call you to ensure you're not likely to waste your time with men who clearly aren't a match.

xi

This book consists of three types of perspectives:

💜 ***Lessons:*** These are specific experiences I thought would be useful to you. A few lines from my experience illustrate the points.

💜 ***Insights:*** These usually start with an experience I've encountered, then the insights that experience spawned. It is usually comprised of around half story and half insight.

💜 ***Stories:*** These are examples of situations I've experienced — or was currently experiencing when I wrote that piece — that I thought would be entertaining. Or I thought the story would help you see what kind of things happen in the midlife dating world so you'd know what has happened to others.

Because these writings were real time, as they occured, they are often set in the present tense. But they are not chronological. So a reference to "my current beau" may now be many sweethearts ago. I hope this isn't confusing.

I'd love ot hear your stories and questions. Please email them to me at Goddess@DatingGoddess.com. They may make it into the blog or my next book!

Who is the Dating Goddess?

I am a middle-aged, white, professional woman. My husband of nearly 20 years left me in April 2003 when I was 47, 11 days shy of 48. After giving my heart time to heal from the surprise divorce sprung by the man I thought was my soulmate, I started dating 18 months later. Generally, I have had a great time meeting interesting men, some of whom became romantic beaus, some became treasured friends, and some I never heard from again.

I am not a well-preserved, gorgeous, marathon-running middle-aged women

In the beginning, I had dates with single male colleagues, but I quickly found Internet dating was the way to explore the most "inventory" and qualify men who I thought might be a good match.

I am not one of those well-preserved, gorgeous,

marathon-running middle-aged women. I have been told I am attractive, but I am overweight and not a gym rat. So while I am active, I do not match the description 90% of men's profiles say they want: slender, athletic, toned, fit. I have some wrinkles — what one sweet suitor mistakenly called dimples. I have what Bridget Jones called "wobbly bits," as most non-surgically enhanced middle-aged women do. My genes — and a lifetime addiction to chocolate — have made their mark. Yet I've met and dated some wonderful men, so even if you're not a lingerie model, you can find guys who will think you're attractive, perhaps even hot!

In my professional life, I am a bestselling author of workplace effectiveness books, professional speaker and management consultant. I've appeared on Oprah, 60 Minutes, and National Public Radio and in the *Wall Street Journal* and *USA Today*.

This book is intended to not only be useful to others and cathartic for me, but is also the genesis of a new topic for fun, thought-provoking speeches. I'm calling myself a dating philosopher and giving date-a-vational speeches! Let me know if you know a group who would like an entertaining after-lunch speech on how lessons learned from dating have implications in business and personal relationships and well as life philosophies.

How did I come by the Dating Goddess moniker? After a few months of dating dozens of men — one week yielded 7 dates with 6 guys in 5 days — my friends dubbed me this name. I liked it, so it stuck.

I'm purposefully not sharing my picture as I don't want you to think either, "How did she get any dates at all?" or the opposite, "Of course she found it easy to get 112 men to ask her out." I am not hideous (usually) nor am I stunning (without professional hair, makeup and Photoshop!). Some men find me attractive, some don't.

I continue to search for my "one," but I have learned a lot along the way, and my single and not-single friends have loudly encouraged me to share my experiences and lessons in the hopes of helping others navigate the adventure of dating with more success. And to have a delicious time doing it!

Make sure to download your free eBook Attract Your Next Great Mate: Dating Advice From Top Relationship Experts *at www. DatingGoddess.com/freebie*

Knight and day

How many women have said they want a "knight in shining armor"? Well, I found one. Literally. His after-work life involves teaching historical swordplay and leather craft. He often gives dueling demonstrations at Renaissance fairs.

He introduced himself by email the other day. (I wonder if it's hard to type while wearing metal gloves. Maybe I should say he chain-mailed me.)

He's also called me twice. (Must be fun to see an armor-wearing, sword-wielding guy on a cell phone.) We jested about jousting and how he could pun in his classes: "Do you get my point?" "This one will slay you."

He seems to be on a crusade to woo me. (Will our first date be at Round Table? Will he pick me up on a white horse?) I think I would like being referred to as "M'Lady" and treated like a queen. His bowing when I enter the room might get old, but I should try it before I decide.

If we move in together, would we buy Costco-sized armor polish? And just how does one launder a cod-piece — in a cold, warm or delicate cycle? Would we get a giant circular table for when his knight-friends visit?

It might be fun to live in a castle, although I rarely see them in the local real estate listings. Would you have to get a variance for a moat?

Would you have to get a variance for a moat?

A modern-day Lancelot has allure, but there would be some barriers (hopefully not hot-oil filled ones). While he has a ready-made Halloween costume, I just don't have the wardrobe to accompany a knight — by day or night. If we were invited to a suit-required event, would I have to specify, "Not the metal one"? Would his tights and mine get confused in the wash?

It would be comforting to know I'd be out with a man who would fight (and no doubt win) if my honor was impugned. But I just don't see myself hanging out at duels. Could I bring my laptop, and would there be a wireless connection?

It seems we are fond of different centuries. Perhaps I'll let this one pass. Or I might just have an ale with him to see if he's as sharp as his sword.

If it didn't work out, I have my exit line ready: "Good knight, good luck"!

Becoming smitten with the fantasy

I've been surprised when men become smitten with me without yet meeting me. Perhaps we've had some interesting emails and phone calls, and they begin professing their love — or lust — for me. It's happened enough times, I've decided it has little to do me — they fall for the fantasy. When I was first dating I did the same thing. Now I'm more savvy.

It is easy to fall for someone absent the reality. You only have blurry or old photos, a few hours — at most — of phone conversation, and some emails. Until you meet, you don't really know if there is a spark, or if there is some annoying habit that is a deal breaker.

A while ago I was contacted on a Tuesday by an intelligent, successful, tall, nice looking, articulate guy. We talked by email and phone a few times over the next few days. He was flirty and suggestive, even leaving one erotic voicemail — all before we'd even met. I warned him that reality was never as good as fantasy.

We set a drink date for Friday. I dressed in nice, sexy casual. He arrived looking nothing like his picture — he left his toupee and glasses at home. However, we had good conversation, and he asked if I'd like to stay for dinner. A good sign. We continued talking about personal history, divorce stories, business, world events. He walked me to the car and left with a hug and quick kiss on the cheek.

I wrote him a nice "thank you" email, as I always do, saying I'd be happy to see him again if he'd like. He sent me a "nice evening; we're not a match" response.

So how did he get from erotic emails to we're not a match? Whatever he fantasized about me wasn't a match for the reality. I have recent, full-length pictures posted in my profile, so he saw what I looked like. So somewhere during our meeting his fantasy fire was extinguished.

Now when I hear someone going overboard before meeting, I know it's a yellow flag. Best to reserve your assessment until you've actually been with someone, and then you need to see them a few times before their "real" self begins to emerge.

Can Google help — or hinder — your dating life?

Perhaps you're like me and immediately Google a guy as soon as you have his first and last name. While I've never found any incriminating evidence this way, I have found some interesting items about the guy I'm considering meeting. I imagine myself a CSI (one of my favorite TV shows), linking disparate clues to complete a puzzle.

Early in my midlife dating adventure, a man with an unusual first name contacted me online. His profile said he was active in our local Rotary Club as well as an organization specific to his lineage.

I Googled the local Rotary Club web site. I searched the site for his first name and voila, a mention appeared including his last name. Armed now with more information, I Googled his full name. I found the web site for the small company he owned, complete with picture

> *I imagine myself a CSI, linking disparate clues to complete a puzzle.*

(which luckily matched the one on the dating site, so I knew he'd posted a reasonably recent one). It gave the company's address, phone number and map. His bio said he'd been president of his national trade association. Nice!

A little more digging found the organization relating to his ancestry. A quick search on the site by his first and last name revealed a listing with his home phone number. Googling that yielded his home address, and a Google map showed me where he lived. If I had wanted to go the next step, Zillow.com would have revealed how much his house was worth (although no info on any mortgages or liens).

This took all of 10 minutes.

Scary, isn't it? Which is why I suggest you be a bit secretive in the beginning of relationships. You don't want a guy you haven't met Googling your home phone number and getting a map to where you live!

I don't typically tell a guy I've Googled him. Some read it as "potential stalker." However, when I have disclosed it after a few dates, most guys seem flattered that I took the time to look, and that I know things about them that they didn't know were on the web.

I Googled a guy I dated for two months who was

a former city official. There was lots of press on him, luckily all good. The reporters were respectful of him. That says a lot.

So I encourage you to Google away. However, keep the findings to yourself unless you uncover something bothersome, then ask him about it. If he squirms, gets upset or avoids your inquiry, then it's probably best to pass on this guy.

Google yourself and see what's out there about you — or someone with the same name.

Getting to know a man through Google

A new man contacted me who held some allure so I promptly did a Google search, armed only with his profile's unusual alias and his city. A wealth of information was divulged.

I read the posting he'd made in public forums so could see his comments were thoughtful, articulate, and had correct spelling and punctuation. I agreed with many of his views. Most of us aren't particularly guarded when we post something to a forum, especially if using an alias. So the fact that he didn't curse or call other posters idiots — as others in the forums did — showed me he had a sense of appropriateness and decorum.

But the most telling information came from his Flickr account. Dozens of photos were on public view. I could tell from what profession he was retired as there were pics of him at work, his hobbies, and photos of him growing up. Thanks to the captions, I saw pictures of his friends, mother, work mates, kids, and past girl-friends! I even learned his last name, which prompted another Google search.

Putting the pictures, captions and forum postings together gave me some tenor of the man. Posing with his arm around his mother and kids sent the impression he was close to them. His comments about his coworkers were positive. The candid shots showed him laughing and having a good time. And his captions describing his past girlfriends divulged to me the kind of woman he was drawn to. (I checked the dates the last girlfriend pics were taken and they were a year old!)

Can you learn everything you need about a person from such sleuthing? Of course not. But such snooping — even if it is in public sties — can show inklings that might have taken longer to experience in person. I will meld this information with his articulate emails with his just-begun brief phone calls and see if I want to get to know this man further. After all, I've done a lot of research on him!

Qualify your potential dates before meeting

Have you learned how to weed out many men who aren't good matches — before meeting them? Why meet and waste both our time if you know ahead of time it's definitely not a match? Men have to go through a few hoops before getting a date with me — even if it's just a coffee date. I've learned to "qualify" my potential dates, and even so, a few got through that I shouldn't have accepted.

There are two main hoops: email and phone.

♥ **Emails:** They have to be engaging ,and he has to appear to have read mine. I've grown fond of men through their emails. I've also been turned off. It's best when the exchange is an ongoing conversation and he refers back to previous emails. It's even better when he's witty, funny, and flirty. I like banter. If his emails are terse, few-word sentences, it doesn't bode well. And if there are too many typos or grammatical errors, it is not good. If the dating site's email system doesn't have spell check and he doesn't care enough to compose in Word and check before sending, a big yellow flag obscures his profile.

Some men take flirty emails to a sexual level. I've had some ask my bra cup size and other extremely personal preferences before even meeting me. Not that it would be OK after meeting me, but presumed intimacy way too early is a deal breaker.

One man's fun, ongoing riff on the goddess theme earned him many points. He even attached goddess pictures and made fun god/goddess references. Since he is a Pisces, he claimed that he was Neptune, which then spawned a series of flirty, "Is that a trident in your pocket, or are you just glad to see me?" comments. I was fond of him before we met and forgave some things that were otherwise deal breakers because of his creative emails.

If his emails are fun and nearly typo-free (I let a few through myself, I know), then he gets my phone number, but only after a few exchanges and/or a few days. People's true colors can come out pretty quickly, and I don't want to give my number to a wacko.

Phone: If the first call is strained and he doesn't know how to have a two-way conversation, I pass on a face-to-face. If he dominates the conversation, I know it doesn't matter if I show up or not, as he's not interested in learning about me. If he's argumentative or condescending, bye bye birdie. If he asks questions like one guy did, "At what point would you feel comfortable getting intimate? The first date?" "No." "The second date?" "No." "The third date?" "Probably not," he's history. If he only talks about things you have no interest in and you can't find some common interest areas, say sayonara.

If he rants about how women lie on their profiles, are too fat, he talks negatively about women in general or how he still fights with his ex, best to bid him farewell before even meeting. If he tells you of his financial woes, or how his ex-wife or ex-girlfriend have him tied up in litigation, best to let this one go. If he is jobless or still lives at home, bon voyage.

Once he passes these hurdles, we can have a coffee date. (See "Start with coffee" in the book *First-Rate First Dates: Increasing the Chances of a Second Date* to understand why.)

How do you qualify your potential dates? What does a guy need to do to earn a date with you?

A tale of two phone calls

While his profile was refreshing and intriguing, our phone conversation was strained. I tried to pull him out by asking questions related to his profile comments. Although he'd initiated contact with me within 24 hours of the call, he asked me nothing about my profile comments, and only asked me one question. He suggested coffee, but I begged off as I didn't feel drawn to invest an hour or two to meet.

He asked nothing from my profile and only asked me one question

However, the next day, I had a long phone conversation with another gentleman. We talked about important lessons from relationships and what we are each looking for. He asked incisive questions and shared his experiences. Soon an hour had whizzed by.

We set a dinner date for later in the week.

What was the difference? It should be pretty clear from the above. The first guy didn't make it easy to converse. He didn't ask me but one question, so I felt like it was a "blind" call even though he'd make the initial contact. The second one asked important questions and shared his perspective, even when it wasn't the same as mine. The second one won the date!

The first time ...
calling him

A guy you've been emailing from a dating site has given you his number and requested you call if you want to talk. You're grateful because you're uneasy giving a stranger your phone number.

His number sits on a Post-It on your desk. You pick it up several times a day. But you put it down each time. Without dialing.

You like his profile and his pic. His emails have been interesting. So why don't you call?

You don't know what to say. You're afraid of stammering and stuttering and sounding like an idiot. You have no trouble making business calls, but this is different. You don't have much practice doing this, since the last time you dated men made the first move. The Internet, stalkers, and safety concerns have changed all that.

So the ball is in your court.

You could always wimp out and write him an email.

Or an IM. Or just give him your number. But no, you want to hear his voice, and yet you're uncomfortable giving out your number, no matter how nice and sane he's seemed so far.

You know you need to dial the phone. But how to start?

Review his profile or whatever you know about him before dialing. If you want a cheat sheet, prepare 3 or 4 open-ended questions. These get people to talk more. They start with how, what, who, why, when and require more than a one- or two-word response. You could start with "Tell me about...," "Help me understand...," "I'm curious about...," "Share with me...," "I'm interested in...."

You could ask questions that elicit a "yes" or "no" answer, but then the conversation can stall. If he's a bit nervous, he won't elaborate. So prompt him with a question that invites him to talk more.

Also, don't interrogate him with rapid-fire questions. Make sure you comment on his response before asking another question. And allow him to ask you some questions. I find it best to end my answers with a question back to him, even if it's just, "What do you think on that topic?"

Here's a sample for you.

You: Hi Mark. This is Sally, also known as Sunny-Bright from Match.com. I wanted to call and say "Hi."

Him: Hi Sally. It's nice to finally hear your voice.

You: Thanks. It's nice to hear yours, too. I liked your profile and I've enjoyed our email exchanges. You are an interesting guy. (A little sincere flattery is a good way to begin. Don't comment on his pic by saying that you think he's cute, as the pic could be from a long time ago. When you meet, he might not look much like his pic.)

(Now ask him an open-ended question. Something from his profile.) I thought it was interesting that you said you were an East Coast transplant. What is the most striking difference you've found from living on both coasts?

(If you said, "Do you like living on the West Coast?" or "Do you miss the East Coast?" he could just answer "yes" or "no.")

Him: The people here are more open and friendly, which is great. I haven't had time to meet a lot of folks, but am getting some friends from work and the sailing club.

You: I remember you said in your profile you liked to sail. I love to sail, too, but haven't been out in a long time. I love the wind on my face and being so close to the water. What's your favorite thing about sailing?

And you're off. On the first call, people commonly ask, "What are you looking for in a romantic partner?" But they often express that in their profile — even if it is typically nebulous. And people aren't particularly willing to go into a deep discussion on the first call. You want to know if you might be a match, but unless he says something that is totally off-putting, you can't really tell if you might be a match or not.

Some women also try to feel out a man's readiness for a committed relationship and his interest in having a family. A guy may say he's ready to settle down, but he doesn't know he isn't until he is in a relationship. So you can ask, but a guy may say what he thinks you want to hear — not because he is purposefully lying (although some will), but because he's not really clear on what he wants and doesn't realize it.

You never know what you're gonna get

The purpose of this first call is to see how easy he is to talk to. If it is difficult to maintain a conversation, it's not good. If he talks 90% of the time about himself, how much money he makes (or the material goods he has that tells you how much money he makes), how horrible his ex is, or curses or gets sexual, then no need to bother meeting. However, most people are on their best behavior on the first call, so if there is nothing odious about him at this point, it's probably worth another call or coffee.

But let him ask! Don't say, "Shall we get together?" or "Do you want to have coffee?" Yes, you're an assertive,

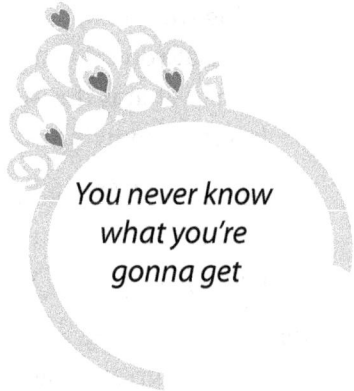

take-charge, Twenty-First Century woman. But this is not the time to show it. It will come out soon enough. You shouldn't be something you're not, but allow him to make the invitation. Unless you're into shy men, he needs to show enough interest — and confidence — to suggest the next contact. Even if he says, "I'm up to my eyeballs in work the next few days. Let me call you back in a day or two," that is a good sign. If you don't want to give your number, say, "No problem. Email me a good time and I'll call you back in a few days."

Failed phone audition

We'd flirted online a few times many months ago, then stopped. I can't remember why. We started again last week. Last night he called. This psychology professor included these tidbits in his 45-minute monologue:

- He told me in great detail of his recent tooth extraction — his third — and his options for implants or a bridge. Why extraction? Because he went to the dentist only every three years (his insurance would pay for every six months) and ignored the infections that caused his teeth to rot.

- He planned his vacations only around time-share pitches at hotels so he could have a free weekend stay.

- He dabbled in day trading, so currently had invested this month's mortgage money and had maxed out his credit card advances to buy a new stock, even though he'd lost money in the past.

- He described the social psychology class he just finished teaching. When he began to explain social psychology, I said, "That was my minor in college." He continued with his explanation as if

I had no idea what it was.

I asked him questions and injected statements — when he took a breath, which wasn't often. There were many times he could have asked me questions about my comments, but he didn't. I tried for 15 minutes to extricate myself, and finally did. He said, "Give me a call when you have a few minutes."
Right. Like that's going to happen.

This call reminded me of a few things:

> *I tried for 15 minutes to extricate myself*

While I try to give people grace, I learned everything I needed to know in 30 minutes that this man was not a fit for me. Anyone who ignores his dental hygiene for three years and repeatedly has teeth removed because of it doesn't have the decision-making skills I'm looking for. This well-paid man is so cheap he only goes on free vacations. If he's gambling with his mortgage money, this is not someone whose values I respect. And finally, if he ignores what I say, he's just interested in a monologue so it doesn't really matter if I'm there or not.

I make assumptions that because someone is

educated, in a certain profession or knows certain information (like psychology), they will behave in a socially astute way. Not necessarily.

💜 I'm glad I have a "phone-call first" rule. If I didn't I'd have taken time to get dolled up and drive to a Starbucks to sit excruciatingly while this man blathered on. Now I won't be making that drive.

💜 I need to be bolder when I want to end a call, perhaps bordering on rude for those who don't pick up on subtler clues.

This experience also made me wonder what I did that caused me to fail phone auditions. It is not only me who has rejected invitations for further contact after a call. Occasionally I'll think a call went swimmingly, never to hear from the guy again.

When you've decided not to see someone after an initial call, what did they do or not do that led you to this decision?

One ringy-dingy —
making the first call
go smoothly

Many people have difficulty with the first phone call. If you are initiating the call, you may procrastinate because you don't know how to start.

Nowadays, men know that some women don't want to give out their number, so they give her their number. This gives the woman more control over who they call and when. But with caller ID, once you've called he has your number.

I like to call first from my cell phone. If you give your land line number, anyone can easily put it in Google and find out not only your street address, but a map to your home!

1.   ***Don't put off calling for more than a few days*** after getting the person's number. It shows you're either not very interested or too busy to see him.

Some waiting is good, but too long and he'll move on.

2. ***Review the person's profile before you call.*** In fact, having it in front of you is a good idea. If he calls you, quickly find his profile if you are in front of your computer so you can be more conversant about him, his interests and life. It is annoying to be asked "Are you divorced," "Do you have kids?" "What city are you in?" and other data that is in my profile.

3. ***Listen carefully.*** This means you shouldn't place the first call while driving, grocery shopping, or other tasks that may distract you. I find it rude if someone I haven't talked to before tries to multi-task during the call. It doesn't make a good first impression. If he calls you and you're caught in the middle of something, ask if you can call him back within a certain time period.

You never know what you're gonna get

4. ***Don't interrupt.*** If you tend to be an interrupter, keep it in check, especially during the first call. I've declined dates with guys who were blatant interrupters, as I find that an annoying habit.

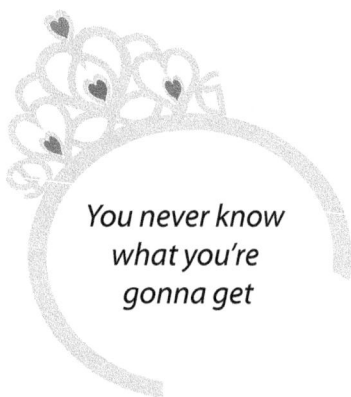

5. ***Ask questions, but don't interrogate.*** Think of questions that will help you know the person better, beyond the basics of profession and employer.

6. ***Share air time.*** A person who hogs the conversation is a bore! Make sure there is give and take, so he feels like you are interested in him.

7. ***Take a deep breath and just dial!***

Who would fall for this?

is French accent was fetching. He laughed immediately which was disarming. We chatted on the phone about life for 20 minutes.

He'd said in his dating site profile that he didn't do coffee dates. I asked him how he met woman initially if he didn't meet for coffee. He said he met them for sex.

> *"What?" I asked incredulously, thinking I must have misheard him through his French accent. He repeated himself. I hadn't misheard.*

> *"You meet women initially for a sex date?" I was too shocked to say anything more intelligent.*

> *"Yes."*

> *"And women do that?"*

> *"Absolutely. It's how we get to know each other."*

> *"Well, then we won't be meeting."*

> *"Why not?"*

"Because I don't have sex with a man I've just met."

"Why not?"

"Because I need to have an emotional connection and trust. That takes time. It doesn't happen on the first date."

"So how has it worked for you to wait? Have those relationships worked out?"

He got me. We wouldn't be talking if any of my relationships had worked out longer than a few months.

"So waiting doesn't really work, does it?"

"Well, I haven't figured out what works. But I know having sex on the first date doesn't work. So it looks like we're at an impasse. You're unwilling to have a non-sex first meeting and I'm unwilling to have a sexual first meeting." And so we said goodbye.

This technique obviously works for this man, at least sometimes, or he wouldn't pursue this approach. I wonder how many women would fall for this line of reasoning.

Are you putting your best voice forward?

Do you know what your voice projects about you to your potential date? Most people don't. They can't even stand to listen to their outgoing voice mail. But in the dating game, how you sound is one component of the dance that can either lead the guy to ask you out or beg off.

Recently I talked to a new potential suitor. His picture was cute; his profile expressed intelligence and humor; he was tall. All good things.

But his voice wasn't as deep and strong as I like. Is it a deal breaker? No. But it doesn't add to his allure. However, another man with a Barry White-type deep, melodious voice earned many dates with me, even though there were other things that weren't a great fit. I loved hearing him speak and overlooked other imperfections because of it.

Another man was jovial on the phone, but he mispronounced too many words, even though he had a graduate degree. He also slurred words. If he'd just had some help with diction and enunciation, he would have come across much better. Another's speech pattern was effeminate. He is intelligent and fun, but when I first heard him on the phone, I wondered if he might be gay. He isn't. I went out with both, so the voice wasn't a show stopper. But it did make a difference in their overall attractiveness.

How you react to someone's voice, like many attributes, is totally subjective. I'm pleased when a man says he likes my voice. One said, "I'm so glad you don't have a high, nasal, or squeaky voice. That would be hard to listen to." I have worked hard to have a pleasant voice, even suffering through listening to recordings of myself to make improvements.

You don't want to sound breathy, as that sounds like you work for a 900 service! I know a woman who answers the phone with a breathy "hel-low," sounding as if she were the receptionist for a call-girl service, rather than a midlife mother of teenagers. And she only talks like that until she knows who it is, then she slips into her "normal" tone. The difference feels odd because of the inconsistency. She does, however, have wrong numbers call back just to chat with her! But none have resulted in a date.

Get some feedback about your voice. If you could improve, get some help from a voice coach. It will not only affect your success in dating, but will probably help you in your job as well.

He makes you laugh — is that enough?

W omen list the number one thing they want in a guy is "someone who makes me laugh." While I agree this is important, it is not the overarching criteria on which to base a relationship.

I was contacted by a guy who had emailed me several months ago. I had sent him one of my nice "thanks but no thanks" emails. He responded:

> *"There are a lot of things missing in my profile that I would like to point out, so since bullet point presentations are what I do on a regular basis, I thought this would give you a better idea of who I am.*

1. *My business is doing very well, so I am financially secure. Since all of this terrorist stuff started, they basically leave the drug dealers alone. As a result it would probably be several months before I try to borrow money from you.*

2. *I am emotionally available. Ever since I was acquitted of my ex-wife's death, all of the issues of*

emotional baggage are safely at the bottom of San Francisco Bay. Literally.

3.   I am of upstanding and forthright character. This can be verified by the type of people that are frequently seen around me: judges, attorneys, miscellaneous members of law enforcement and parole officers.

4.   I have been clean and sober for almost six weeks now. Unfortunately I need to admit that I have put on a few pounds since giving up heroin as my diet aid.

5.   I was given a clean bill of health by the instructor of the anger management course that I was required to take (these court ordered things are so annoying). The instructor mentioned that he has never seen such a radical and permanent change in any student ever. Ironically I was punching him when he said that, but you get the general drift of what I'm trying to say.

6.   As a father, I have instilled excellent values in my children. My son was recently arrested and refused to rat out his co-defendants. Even after they offered to let him walk.

Humor can tilt the scale in a guy's favor.

Makes a father feel proud to see his son living by a code. My daughter has really taken my business sense and gone to a whole new level. She currently has about eight girls working for her. They are doing great. I don't get to see her as often as I like, due to her business being only legal in Nevada. She has considered moving back to California, but seems to think L.A. is the appropriate place. There appears to be some significant market share since Heidi Klum left the business.

"Ok — so I am trying to make you laugh."

Did he make me laugh? Yes. Did I agree to a date? No. There were too many things in his profile that were unappealing that even a great sense of humor couldn't overcome. However, if there was only one or two things that weren't a fit, I would have considered it based on his humor and persistence. So humor can tilt the scale in a guy's favor. But it alone is not enough. Be clear on your criteria and if humor is one item, don't allow it to overshadow all others.

Make sure to download your free eBook Attract Your Next Great Mate: Dating Advice From Top Relationship Experts at www. DatingGoddess.com/freebie

Getting to know a man through his humor

A recent press release announced a new dating site, Funny Passions, for "singles with a sense of humor."

This strikes me as odd. I've never met anyone who thought him/herself humorless. Nearly everyone thinks they have a sense of humor, even if it's obscure.

Why is this site different? The release says it's "an entire site focused exclusively on bringing together people who consider a sense of humor to be important in their friendships and in their romantic relationships." Doesn't everyone think humor is important to their relationships? So what's the big deal here?

The release says they bring together like-humored folks, "a few of the groups on the site are Amateur Comedian, British Humor, Camp, Dry Sense of Humor, Political Humor, Sarcastic, Slapstick, Twisted and Life of the Party. It will be easier to find others who can make them laugh, and who 'get their jokes.' While everyone enjoys a good laugh, it's also great when you find others who you can make laugh."

While I agree that laughing and making others laugh is important, laughter is not the only thing that determines compatibility. In "He makes you laugh — is that enough?" (page 35), I talked about how a man's ability to make you laugh can block out deal breakers if you let it. One man I met online makes me laugh like no other. Yet we are not a match in other areas. We have transitioned to friends so we can enjoy the parts of each other we like and not get irritated with the parts that make us not a match.

Humor can be a way to avoid talking about deeper, serious topics. If someone is always making a crack when you're trying to be soulful, it can get annoying. I wonder, "What's he hiding? Is he uncomfortable talking about this?" I'll ask if he's uneasy, and if he still tries to hide behind humor, I know we're not a match.

Humor is sometimes an attention-getting device. Think of the class clown — s/he got a lot of attention from being funny. I know that was part of my motivation for taking that role. But if someone is not willing to relinquish the spotlight — if he is always "on" — it can get old.

Also, if he doesn't laugh at your attempts at humor, it shows that it's all about him being the focus. Humor can be a form of control. He likes it when he makes you laugh. If you can get someone to do something involuntarily, it is a powerful position. Why do comedians get paid so much? Because they let us leave our worries behind in a pleasurable way. They make us laugh.

I look for the tone of the humor. If it is focused on making fun of others, it can be a form of aggression. If his cracks make fun of you, it can be a way to express anger that he doesn't know how to communicate openly and maturely. Humor, at someone else's expense, can be abuse.

I look for the tone of the humor

Not to say funny people are self-centered powermongers and control freaks. But in excess, this can be true.

I like occasional self-deprecating humor, but if all the jokes are Woody Allen-like, it can be a sign of low self-esteem. I like people who are confident and humble — people who can laugh at themselves, but not always putting themselves down.

The art of consideration

When most guys are starting to woo a woman, they work to make her happy. They do things that they think will show they are considerate and care. They suggest activities they think she'll like.

I've dated guys who were very considerate. One said, "You pick the movie/restaurant and I'll pay," to show he was flexible. Others have brought small gifts they think I'll like or suggested movies or restaurants they are pretty certain I'd like. This goes a long way in the wooing department.

However, ask yourself if what he thinks is considerate matches your definition. One potential suitor called me every day, which I'm sure he thought showed he was considerate. Unfortunately, he called me at 7:00 a.m. on

> *He called me every day, which I'm sure he thought was considerate*

43

his way to work. I am not a morning person. So he awakened me, then chastised me for being a sleepy-head. He bedded down at 9:00, I go to bed between 11 and midnight. So he was bright eyed at 5:30. I was not.

So even though I explained to him that I am not a morning person, he continued to call when it's convenient for him, not me.

While I gave him grace and thought about his point of view — that he was being considerate — I finally concluded that he wasn't listening when I told him he awakened me, so he was not being considerate. I think consideration is a foundation to a positive relationship. So I finally told him not to call me — no matter what the time!

Anticipating a big date is like awaiting Santa

I was excited to finally be meting a man with whom I'd been communicating for a month, with nearly daily hour-long phone calls. I felt like a kid on Christmas Eve, unsettled with the excitement of what Santa will bring. Do you remember that feeling of joyous anticipation as you await a big event?

I pondered, will the electricity be as great in person as it has been on the phone? Will he look like his pictures? What if he doesn't like how I look? What if I don't like the real-life version as much as I've liked the virtual version? Will it be better than I imagine or worse?

It takes will power not to build up impossible expectations, which lead to inevitable disappointments. Trying to be Zen, "Whatever is is," feels unattainable. Singing "Whatever will be will be," trite.

"Why, I wondered to myself, "is this meeting so different than previous first encounters?" First, we'd connected deeply for a month, talking about things that matter: goals, fears, feelings, accomplishments, mistakes, regrets. This creates pent-up expectations. Second, this man behaved differently than any of his predecessors. In fact, he'd been so unlike any of the others, I waived my "locals only" rule since he lives 2000 miles away. How would we ever develop a relationship long distance? How can that possibly work? Yet I know that if two people want something to work, they will be very creative to make it happen.

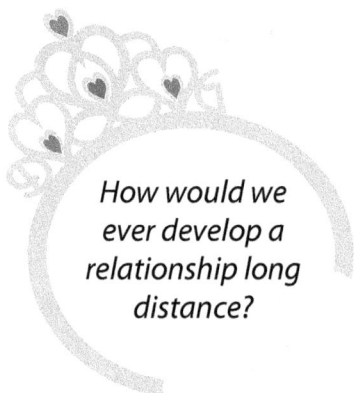

> *How would we ever develop a relationship long distance?*

So I waited for the appointed time, busying myself with work to keep my mind occupied. I started getting ready way before I really needed to. I didn't want to be rushed. I wanted to look my best. I didn't want to be stressed with little setbacks — run in the stockings, changing outfits to choose the right one, heavier-than-usual traffic. I wanted to be relaxed and stress free for this big date. Wouldn't you?

I was caught up in wondering what surprises Santa would bring.

"What are you wearing?"

I've been asked this on the phone by more than one potential suitor. Sometimes he's met me, but more often he hasn't. I've decided it's part of the fantasy he's creating.

What does he want me to say? The truth — gardening togs? Baggy sweats and warm socks? Flannel nightie and fuzzy slippers? I tried telling the truth and noticed the conversation deflated.

So now I play. "Nothing," or "Only a smile" I'll reply to see his response. There is usually some incredulousness. Sometimes I say, "What do you want me to be wearing?" After he tells me I say, "How did you guess?" I give him what he wants to hear — and imagine. ☺

A male friend says since most men are visual, they want to imagine you in something sexy and slinky. From Victoria's Secret. My pal says I should respond, "A black lace teddy," or "a red silk negligee" — as if many women actually lounge around the house alone in such attire. I'm sure some do, as I read Mariah Carey claims to. None of my midlife women friends do — or at least none have shared that they do.

I think women rarely ask this question of a guy because we don't really want to hear "sweats" or "shorts and a t-shirt." If we're interested in him, we want to imagine the guy in a nice shirt and slacks, well-fitting jeans and polo shirt, silk boxers, or whatever floats your boat. So best not to ask if you don't want to know the truth.

Have you been asked what you're wearing? If so, what do you respond? Have you asked a guy what he's wearing? Why?

Being seduced by what he is over who he is

I admit it. I've been so enticed by what a man is that it's clouded my judgment about who he is.

When dating the crazy psychiatrist, I adored when he consulted the pharmacist about what over-the-counter remedy would reduce my cold symptoms. I loved telling my friends that I was dating a doctor. Shallow, I know. Very shallow. I felt like his profession meant that I was able to attract smart, accomplished men. I ignored the ever-present fact that he was a self-admitted "impaired physician," meaning a doctor with problems. And he had those in spades. If he'd been a normal guy — engineer, Realtor, manager, contractor — I wouldn't have put up with the junk he threw at me.

The Academy Award winner was similar. His accomplishment overrode telling signs that this man wasn't for me. But I was enthralled with the prospect of attending private screenings and Oscar night with him. I told myself, "I deserve someone who is at the top of his field," even though he'd earned the award as part of a stellar team, not an individual effort, and that was over 10 years ago.

Luckily, I've not always fed my ego and blinded my assessment by the status of my dates. I wasn't beguiled by the former professional football player, ex pro basketball player, high-tech exec, CEO, lawyer, or venture capitalist.

Sometimes I wish I didn't know a man's accomplishments or profession until I know him better. It is difficult to mask, however, because many list it in their profile or mention it in early communications. I've considered asking a man not to tell me for a while and see if I like him for who he is, not what he is. But now they are intertwined.

It would be like getting to know someone through only email and phone, then showing up to meet him with you both wearing blindfolds. How different your impressions would be without the visual! You could smell his cologne, feel his hand and arm, perhaps hug. Would a kiss be more delicious or less if you didn't know what he looked like?

Do you find yourself entranced by a man's profession and accomplishments? If not, how do you set aside whatever status you attribute to it and allow the man's characteristics to show through?

"I want to court you"

These words are heart melting to a woman who wants love, romance, and a long-term relationship. No other man had said these to me. They were said after two weeks of nightly talking for hours about things that were important to each of us. What broke up past relationships, what was important to each of us, what we were looking for in a mate, what made us happy and unhappy.

I was ready to be courted so was delighted when he said it. I interpreted it as he was romantic, wanted to make me happy, and had long-term intentions.

How do you know if you are ready to be courted? He seemed to have so much of what I was looking for. He was funny, smart, accomplished, asked questions no one else seemed to care about, was interested in getting to know the real me. I was ready to fall in love. After many hours of talking on the phone, we seemed so compatible. I was ready to focus on one person, having grown weary of dating around.

Did he court me? Yes. Coming a 5-hour drive away, we agreed he'd visit my city for a few days. He reserved a hotel room and we met for dinner the first night. We hit it off immediately. We both thought the other was more attractive than the pictures in our profiles. We held hands and cuddled while enjoying a cocktail. We couldn't take our eyes off each other at dinner. We later strolled to another nice bar and lingered over a night cap, not wanting to let each other go. We felt we'd known each other a long time. He said he hadn't felt like this in a long, long time. Was this the love I'd been waiting for?

Was this the love I'd been waiting for?

His courtship had begun in earnest. He was doing and saying all the right things.

The next day we enjoyed each other's company with lots of laughter, deep conversation and cuddling. The following day evolved deliciously with late-morning coffee, exploring art galleries, enjoying the sunset's flaming sky, and dining at a restaurant we discovered was a favorite for both of us. He was good at spoiling me and having fun.

Did his wooing work? Yes and no. Generally, he was a good date, making sure I had what I needed to make me happy. However, while he was doing all of the above, there were also behavioral gnats gnawing at my patience. Was I being an ingrate for all the time and money he invested in showing me a good time? Was I being too sensitive? Too picky? No one was perfect.

Could I live with these minor irritations? I know I have my own set of peculiarities that he would have to adapt to.

We spent a lot of time together over 3 days. When you do, the annoyances mount up. With in-town suitors, you have lunch or dinner together, or spend an afternoon or day in an activity. Then you are apart for a day or more. It gives you a chance to give each other some grace and space. But by spending so much time together in just a few days, the irritants compound.

Will his courtship continue? That is yet to be determined. We both need to decide if the things we enjoy about each other outweigh the burrs. Was there enough positive to invest more time on the phone and in person and see if we can work out the irritations? We will give each other some time to reflect and see what transpires.

Persistence pays —
perhaps

When I first began to date, two men contacted me the same week from the only online site on which I was listed. Each emailed me several times a day the first week, and we spoke by phone. I liked them both, but Mr. JohnnyOnTheSpot asked for a date within the week. The other lived an hour away and it took him three weeks to ask for a date. I agreed to meet him for dinner, although I was already fond of Mr. JohnnyOnTheSpot.

His flirty attitude was gone

Mr. Procrastinator and I had exchanged flirty emails and on the phone he was interesting and complimentary. However, other than a "You're beautiful" when we sat down, his flirty attitude was gone. He was businesslike in his voice tone and discussion topics. He was reserved and rarely smiled. The deep, melodious, sexy voice he used on the phone was now higher pitched. I didn't feel drawn to him in person.

He called the next day and asked me to rate the date on a 1-10 scale. I had decided I really didn't want to see him again, but rather than tell him a 4, I rated it a 7. He acted crushed! I also told him I had begun seeing Mr. JohnnyOnTheSpot. He said he was disappointed, but he understood and wished me well.

A month later he emailed asking how I was doing and how it was going with Mr. JohnnyOnTheSpot. I politely responded that it was going fine. He kept in touch every month and seemed elated when after a few months I told him I had broken up with Mr. JohnnyOn-TheSpot. He called me that day and I warmed to him again, so I started seeing him. So sometimes persistence pays off!

He called me every day for six months, but I only saw him every 10-12 days. He kept promising he'd come see me tomorrow, but something else nearly always took priority. I got tired of being home alone on too many Saturday nights, while he kept professing his devotion to me. So while he was persistent, his actions weren't congruent with his words.

Are you his spare?

For a few weeks a gal pal was exchanging flirty emails multiple times a day with an online match. He then suggested they have dinner and she countered that she was more comfortable with lunch. They continued their multiple-per-day email flirting a few more weeks, but he never again brought up getting together.

She was flummoxed. What was going on?

Two explanations came to me:

1. He enjoyed flirting, but not actually meeting women. This happens more than one would think. Some people just want pen pals, which is perfectly fine as long as they are upfront about it. Leading someone on when you have no intention of meeting isn't right. But he had suggested dinner, so we didn't think he was just a serial flirter.

2. He was trolling for a "spare" woman. Not necessarily a woman on the side if he was married or in a relationship. But more likely he was seeing someone already, but not seriously. So he was still hunting, seeing if there was someone

"better" out there. He wasn't unhappy with his current woman, but he was not so enthralled that he was sure she was "the one." My friend was intriguing enough to flirt with, but not yet enticing enough to press to meet her. (If he did meet her he'd see how fabulous she is!) He was ensuring his pipeline was full in case his current woman dumped him or he lost interest in her.

How do you know if you are his spare? Mostly it will be in the lack of action he takes to meet with you, not only the first time but in subsequent communications. In "Are you getting prime time from your man?" I outline ways you can tell if you aren't a top priority for a guy. While one would think most of these signs are obvious, the haze of infatuation affects us all so we miss signals that are otherwise apparent.

What should you do if you suspect he is stringing you along as his spare — or potential backup?

> *What should you do if you suspect he is stringing you along?*

Limit the time you are willing to put into communicating before meeting. Many Adventures in Delicious Dating After 40 readers agree that you should strive to meet after 2 weeks or less of email exchanges. After that, no matter how much he says he likes you, if there is no effort to meet, even if long distance, there

is not a lot of interest. Too many women have shared they've had extensive email exchanges which turned to naught when they met. You don't want to waste your time, unless you just want a pen pal.

Ask him point blank if he is seeing other women. If he stammers and stutters, "Yes, but no one serious," then you need to decide if you want to meet — or continue to see — him. If you are multi-dating yourself, then maybe it's not a problem for you. But if you believe in dating only one man at a time, you need to tell him your criteria, and if you are interested in meeting him in the future when he's unencumbered, tell him to let you know when he is available.

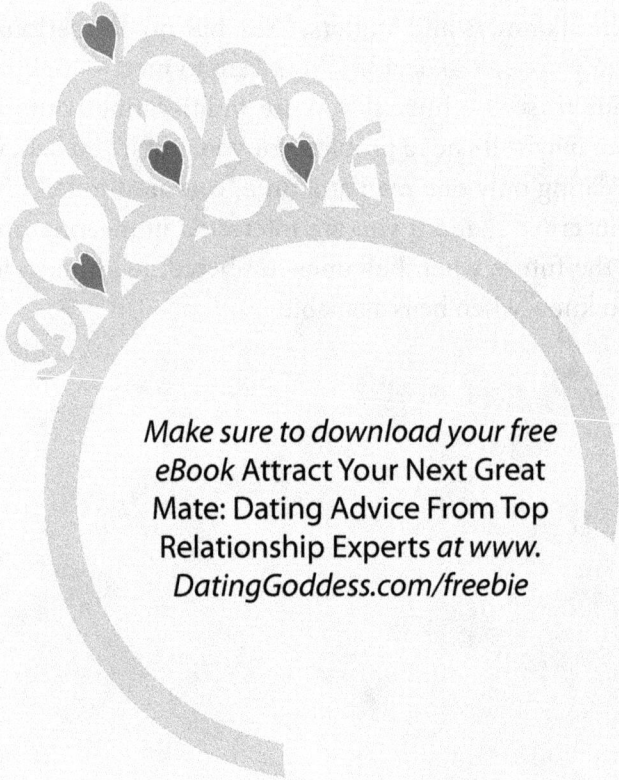

Make sure to download your free eBook Attract Your Next Great Mate: Dating Advice From Top Relationship Experts *at www. DatingGoddess.com/freebie*

The dangers of IM flirting

I'm told some people found the love of their life through an online dating chat room. Others have shared they got to know their beloved long distance through Instant Messages (IMs).

While IMs can be a way to get to know each other quickly, it can also create a false intimacy. I rarely open my IM application because I've found it is easy for men (and I'm guessing women) to get into too personal matters too quickly.

For example, I was checking my matches on a new site that has an automatic IM capability as soon as you log on. Within 30 seconds, a guy said hi to me. I typically ignore these, but he had a nice opening salvo, so I quickly looked at his profile, saw he was out of the area and 20 years younger, so sent him my nice brush off message. He continued asking me about things in my profile. So I decided to be nice and chat with him for a few minutes.

By minute two he was asking me questions that were inappropriate. I told him so, and said if he met me at a party he would not be asking these questions. Then I logged off.

The anonymity of the Internet can encourage some people to say things they wouldn't say in person. Or maybe guys like this would! But I think most would have more of a filter for appropriateness. In email, you have some time to think about what you're writing. But an IM is just that — instant — with very little filtering going on.

This IM assumed intimacy has been more the rule than the exception. If you want to continue to chat you have to tell them your boundaries. But I find if a guy goes sexual in an IM, he's not really someone I want to know more.

And it's not just sexual comments or questions that are a problem. It's easy to share details and feelings with someone you're not looking at face-to-face. "What's wrong with that?" you ask. "Isn't that a great way to get to really know someone?" Yes, it can be. It can also create an imagined attraction when you haven't even met yet. Then when you do and there's no spark, you realize you've fallen for the fantasy that you imagined, rather than the real person.

The good news is if you start IMing with someone who becomes inappropriate and you share your boundaries and he doesn't stop, you can block him from contacting you. Best to nip it in the bud before he has your phone number or address.

Is it neediness, loneliness, or pent up love?

Some men start with sugary sweet talk even before a face-to-face meeting. Some of them try to soften me up, thinking I'll then be an easy mark on the first date for a roll in the hay.

But others don't hint at sex, and say sweet, romantic things in email or on the phone. I've generally written off this sweet talk as neediness, or just the expressions of lonely men.

> It might have something to do with the man aching to love someone

Now I'm wondering if it might also have something to do with the man aching to love someone, to shower her with affection, to pamper and spoil her, starting with his expressions of care. When he finds someone who is nice, communicative and apparently receptive to his verbal kindnesses, he is so overjoyed, he thinks he is smitten. But he hasn't even met the object of desire yet.

I think many people have a lot of love to give, and they get satisfaction from giving love. They give to their family and friends, but yearn for a romantic partner to act out their definition of themselves as a romantic, loving mate. After all, without someone with which to actually be romantic, you are just a theoretical romantic, not a practicing one. If you call yourself a romantic but have no one to romance, your definition of yourself can become shaky.

So are neediness and pent up love the same? The dictionary says "needy" is "lacking the necessities of life." One could easily argue that giving or receiving love is a necessity. So lacking the ability to fully experience love is indeed needy.

Now when a man writes sweet things, unaccompanied by sexual innuendo, I give him some grace. I wait to assess if it is out of his neediness, loneliness or pent up love.

The power of spelling

An Adventures in Delicious Dating After 40 reader brought it up in a comment recently. I and others have mentioned it before. During a TV interview about on-line dating, a fifty-something single woman said it was a pet peeve.

Spelling.

Or more accurately, misspellings. (Spell check told me that "misspellings" was wrong, but Dictionary.com says it's okay.)

On one hand, you can say this is nitpicking, as shallow as complaints about table manners and wrinkled clothing.

On the other you can say multiple email or profile typos show carelessness and cluelessness about early impressions.

Spell check has become so commonplace we can't imagine someone not employing it. However, some dating sites don't have it available in their compose-message boxes. Some email software allows you to enable or disable it. And some people are in such a hurry, they don't notice those red-underlined words.

It seems meticulous spellers have little tolerance for "creative" spellers. And the latter think the former are a tad bit anal retentive. I am on the fence. I am not naturally a good speller, although ironically I always got an A on my spelling tests. Seems I learned for the test, but then promptly forgot. And I'm not good at remembering the rules of grammar, either. But as an author, publisher and even editor, I've had to sear in my mind some common grammar mistakes that are easily overlooked.

> *Meticulous spellers have little tolerance for "creative" spellers*

Does this mean my dating emails are flawless? Heavens no! So I should give my potential suitors a bit more slack since I am afflicted with the same malady.

This has taught me to compose any dating-site email in Word and spell check it before copying and pasting into the site's message box. Of course, this is much easier when the site emails come through your own email box, but not all do.

Curiously, we allow people more leeway in IMs and text messages. The challenge comes when someone employs text message shortcuts (e.g., "u" for "you," "2" for "to," "R" for "are," "8" for "ate") in regular emails.

Most of us midlifers don't find that acceptable, although younger people think it's fine. In fact, I've heard some use those shortcuts in business emails as well!

So what to do? I think it's common sense: Be on your best behavior at first until you've built up a "slack bank" — you've shown you are intelligent, conscientious, and educated. Then if you slip now and then, he will know it was an anomaly. Also, be conscious of the recipient. If careful spelling and grammar is important to him, then reread your emails before hitting send. And it couldn't hurt to ask about his spelling sensitivity level — maybe he doesn't really notice your slips. Unless they are black lace and silk. ☺

My boyfriend, whom I haven't met

A man has been wooing me for six weeks, first via email while I was abroad, then during daily phone calls, emails and/or text messages.

We haven't met, however, because three days after I returned home, he was called to his dying mother's side 2000 miles away. While the doctors told him she only had a few days left, she lived two weeks, only passing the other day. This week he's finishing her burial plans and awaiting the rest of the family's arrival for her funeral next weekend.

We've gotten close during this time, discussing important topics as we've shared stories of our childhoods and parental influences on us. I'm getting to know his values by what he talks about and what he asks me.

If we had met — assuming we hit it off after meeting — I might consider him my beau. He certainly behaves beau-like — at least as much as one can long distance — calling me every day, asking about my life, values and opinions. But this is backwards — usually people get closer after meeting. I've done this before — become close to a man via weeks of phone and email, then when we met, zippo. No connection or chemistry. So I'm working to not get attached to him until we meet.

It's always a quandary to give a word to this type of relationship. Not boyfriend. Not beau. Wooer? When I saw a bunch of my friends this weekend, they asked, "Are you seeing anyone special?" I'd stammer, "I'm being wooed by an interesting man, but we haven't had a date yet." I could have easily said, "Yes, I have a boyfriend whom I haven't met."

But the challenge bigger than what to call him is how much to allow myself to feel connected to him. It seems like jump starting an intimacy that usually begins with meeting and a mutual agreement to get to know each other better.

So to keep from getting too attached I continue to entertain inquiries from men who meet my criteria. I'm slated to have coffee with two new men this week. By not putting all my eggs in one man-basket, I think I'll be better able to assess my connection with the mystery man when we meet next week.

Have you ever become attached to someone after weeks of regular chatting? If so, how did you keep yourself from getting too attached, knowing you had to meet face-to-face before determining if you wanted to invest more energy and emotion?

Too-intimate first contact

An Adventures in Delicious Dating After 40 reader asks:

> *What is your sense about men who react to your online profile with a gushing email about how you are probably 'the one' for them, etc. and also who make several references to making love, the afterglow, etc. I feel uncomfortable if a man seems to idealize me without ever meeting me...and also with references to sex, though I certainly like sex...but somehow it seems a bit out-of-form to bring it up in an introductory email. What is your take on all this?*

Your instincts are right on. If a man idealizes you before he even meets you, he is reacting to a fantasy, not you. He makes up how you are, all from a few words on a profile and a two-dimensional picture. I wrote about this in "Becoming smitten with the fantasy" (page 3).

> *He makes up how you are, all from a few words on a profile*

Most people who are online dating are either lonely or horny or a combination of both. Some more than others. When someone idealizes you without having talked to or met you, they are showing their emotional state — not one you want to travel to! If he talks about sex in the first email, he has no social savvy and will try to get you in the bed the first date. Not a formula for a pleasant time.

So unless you, too, want a quick fling, I'd release guys who do this by sending a "Thanks, but no thanks" email.

When canceling is the right thing to do

You were contacted online by a man who lives 75 minutes away. You exchange a few emails; you have a nice phone conversation. You accept his coffee invitation for a few days hence, agreeing to meet half way.

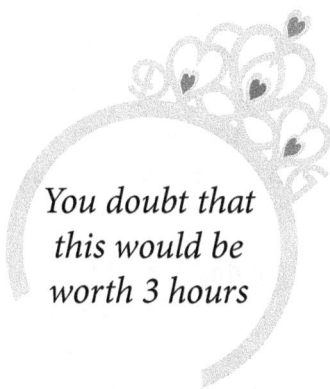

You doubt that this would be worth 3 hours

You think about the conversation for a few days, realizing he disclosed a few things that make you know you aren't a good match in terms of temperament and interests, plus there's the distance issue. You think about the time it will take — 30 minutes to get ready, 45 minutes to drive there, 30-60 minutes for coffee, 45 minutes to drive home. You realize you don't have enough evidence that this would be worth three hours to meet this guy.

You realize it would most likely be a waste of time for both of you.

You take a deep breath and call him and politely cancel.

This is the right thing to do. It is respectful of both of you.

While I typically advocate meeting new men who meet your key criteria, this man doesn't meet enough of what you're looking for. The distance alone would give you pause even if he offered to make the trip most of the time. Yes, distance can be overcome if enough major criteria are met. But with some of what he disclosed on the phone, it sounds like you're not really well matched.

People often tell me how much courage it takes to date. Yes, it takes courage to keep putting yourself out there, meeting new people, risking heartbreak. But it also takes courage to not try to start something with someone you don't have a good sense has the values you're looking for, even if he seems like a nice person.

Yes, this story happened to me this week. I felt bad for a few seconds, thinking I had led him on by accepting his invitation to meet. But then, once I decided I needed to cancel and made the call, I knew it was the right thing for both of us.

Dodging a bullet

I'm becoming pickier as I date longer. In the beginning I'd have coffee with nearly anyone who asked, as long as he was polite, could spell reasonably well in his profile and emails, and didn't curse or get sexual.

However, now that the thrill has worn off of meeting an avalanche of new men, I'm more discerning about to whom I'll give my time. I encourage you to find a balance between meeting interesting new people and weeding out those who clearly aren't a fit before committing to even coffee.

A few days ago I was contacted by a new man from a dating site. His profile was articulate and well written, but I was troubled that his main photo showed a man 10 years younger than another clearly more recent photo he'd posted. A bit of bait and switch, I'd say. Did the gray-haired gent not realize he looked considerably older than the dark-haired man in his primary photo?

After a few email exchanges — some of his were completely in all caps, a pet peeve of mine — he asked about getting together. I ignored this question the three times he asked it, answering others. I wasn't sure I wanted to agree to get together yet.

Finally, I offered that we chat by phone first. We exchanged numbers and I suggested we talk that evening. He informed me he went to bed at sunset and arose at sunrise. I guess that means we wouldn't ever go clubbing — unless it's in Alaska in the summer! And what about when the winter sun sets here at 4:30? Does he have dinner at 4:00? Or maybe he hibernates all winter.

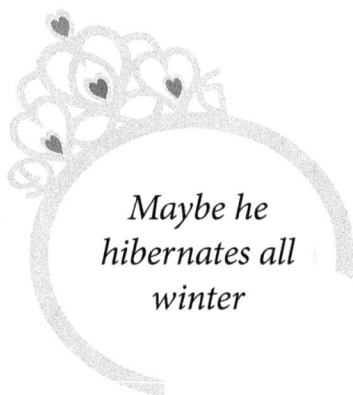

Maybe he hibernates all winter

I said to call when he felt like it and if I was available I'd answer. He called a little after sunset at 7:45. I told him I was surprised to hear from him after dark as I thought he'd be in bed. He said he was!

Throughout the 45-minute call, there were several signs we weren't a match. Ten minutes into the call, I lost him. The phone hadn't disconnected, but there was total silence. I said his name a few times to no response. I hung up. A few minutes later he called back, saying his son called on the other line. He couldn't have said, "Listen, my son is calling; can I call you right back?" No, he just took the call without mentioning it to me!

He proceeded to bash a few organizations and individuals I hold dear. He complained that one thought leader I admire was arrogant, then made a racial slur about him. He was negative about his past wives, even though the most recent divorce was 8 years ago! He said in the 8 years he's been dating he'd only found one woman his intellectual equal — and she was messed up!

He asked little about me, and when he did and I began to answer, he interrupted. Not good social skills.

So when my phone said my battery had 30 seconds left, I informed him of this and bid him adieu. I won't be having coffee with this man — ever.

You learn so much about a man even in a brief conversation. On the phone you aren't distracted by his looks, so you can really hear what he talks about, his view of the world, and how interested he is in knowing about you. You can't tell if someone is a good fit, but you can often tell that he isn't. If there are no red flags, go ahead and have coffee. But if there are things you hear or feel that don't sit well with you, pass on spending time getting together.

Politics, religion and sex — oh my!

Traditional advice tells you to steer clear of these three topics early in a dating relationship. But after a man asked me on a first date to briefly describe my attitude about each of these issues, I saw the wisdom of broaching them right away.

He'd shared with me that on a first date with a doctor, she got embarrassed at the use of the word "sex." After a dozen phone conversations, emails and IMs with him and during our coffee date, I experienced him as a gentleman, never salacious or raunchy, so I doubted he had been with her. By her reaction, both verbal and nonverbal, he deduced she was uncomfortable discussing the subject philosophically, even though he wasn't asking her preferences or experience, just her general attitude. It told him she was not as relaxed about the topic as he needed in a sweetheart. He didn't date her again.

I saw the need to understand a potential suitor's position on politics when having a drink with a man who hadn't listed a political preference in his profile.

We were having a nice time until politics entered the discussion. He commented that a current high-ranking politician was one of the most brilliant men ever in that position. I nearly spit my wine across the table since this was the most ridiculous assessment I'd ever heard. I laughed, as I thought surely he was being sarcastic. He wasn't. It was good to find out that we had 180-degree opposite political perspectives and we needn't waste any future time getting to know each other.

Some couples like James Carville and Mary Matalin can endure having opposite political points of view, but I would grow weary constantly debating such polar perspectives. You can agree not to discuss them, of course, but it would be hard for such glaring differences not to leak out.

> I would grow weary constantly debating such polar perspectives

For six months I dated a man with very different religious views. At first it wasn't an issue, but as we got to know each other more he insisted I go to confession — even though I'm not Catholic — to cleanse my sins. When I informed him I was not going to confession, he told me he was concerned because he didn't want my soul to go to hell. He could not understand how anyone could believe differently. Needless to say, this was a part of why I broke off our relationship — not that we had different religious practices, but that there wasn't room for each others' beliefs.

When the gentleman asked my overview of the three topics, I saw that he was trying not to waste either of our time if we felt the others' perspective was a deal breaker. He shared his point of view as well, and we both were fine about the others' position.

I now try to initiate a similar discussion before I agree to meet a man. I don't want minute details on his sexual preferences, political leanings, or religious practices, but if his overview tells me he is off the scale of my comfort level, best to not even meet. I've been disappointed when I've taken time to learn about a man and meet him — or even date him for weeks or months — then learn he has views or practices that are repellent to me — especially if he expects me to participate in them.

He sends you naughty pics — before you've met!

Salacious. Risqué. Erotic. Nekked.

You didn't request them. He didn't ask if you wanted them. He just sent them. Of him — or various parts of him.

When men have done this it makes me scratch my head. If I were only looking for a roll in the hay, then perhaps seeing the "goods" ahead of time might hasten the arrangements for a meeting. But since I want the whole package, these pics are off-putting. It does, however, give me a very clear picture of what he wants — even when the picture of the goods is a bit blurry.

He sends you pics of various parts of him

A friend told me he communicated for a few weeks

with an out-of-state woman he'd met on a mainstream dating site. She told him she wanted to show him something. She turned on her web cam and did a strip tease for him. He said at first it was titillating, but then he felt voyeuristic. He felt strange and declined her offer to do another for him. She even sent him a web cam so he could do the same for her!

She requested he send a pic of a specific body part. Wanting to appease her, he whipped out his digital camera and tried to find the right angle, lighting and background. He snapped away but nothing worked. After a while, he felt dumb trying to capture a part of him he's not used to seeing in the view finder in order to send it to a stranger. He abandoned his effort, much to her dismay.

Men have asked me for erotic pictures before our first meeting. They typically ask if I have "other" pictures in addition to those on the dating site. This tells me it's not worth even having a meeting as they are singularly focused.

A man said he was going to send me some pictures and hoped I wouldn't be offended. I said, "If you think I might be offended, don't send them. If you wouldn't show them to me on a first date, don't show me now, as we haven't even had a first date." He got it.

So if a man sends or asks for naked pics, just turn this negative into a positive by ending contact.

Two strikes — he's out!

I know — usually it's three strikes before someone is out. But in dating sometimes all you need is two interactions with a man to decide he's out.

Tonight was a good example. A man from a dating site looked at my profile every day for the last two weeks. In his picture, he wore a hat, sun glasses and had written nearly nothing in his profile. However he was height, age and geographically appropriate. He emailed a funny message 5 days ago. I responded with some banter. He replied with his number.

I waited a day to call. I decided to see if he was as funny live as he was in his email. Sometimes yes, sometimes no. At the end of the 30-minute call I thought I would just release him back into the dating pool. However, he wrote a nice email afterward saying how much he enjoyed our call and looked forward to talking again. Yesterday, he emailed asking if I'd call him since I hadn't given him my number. I said I was tied up until

Was he as funny live? Yes and no.

85

late. He emailed today asking if I wanted to have coffee this afternoon. I responded that I was booked, suggesting perhaps tomorrow. He asked if I'd call him tonight to discuss it.

I tried to figure out if he was needy or lonely, or if I should just give him some slack. Since I like to give people some grace, I gave him another chance and called him again tonight. After 10 minutes, I remembered why I was going to let it go after our last conversation.

He would frequently change the subject to some rambling thought. Was he ADHD? Or just an unconscious communicator? He focused on himself (are we surprised?) until he realized he was monopolizing the conversation, then asked me one of the questions he'd asked me just two nights before. Were my answers so uninteresting he couldn't remember from just 48 hours before? When I began to answer, he'd interrupt to share some stream-of-consciousness babble.

When he asked when I could meet him for coffee I made some excuse about having a full schedule for the next few days. Luckily, his self-distraction played to my favor and he changed the subject. I soon excused myself.

Have you found that two interactions are often sufficient to decide if you have enough of a connection to warrant a meeting? Sometimes it doesn't take three strikes for someone to be out.

Up close to a flimflam man

They are out there. We know it. We hope we will be lucky enough to avoid them. But sometimes they come into our lives.

I encountered one up close last night. I met him online. Before you launch into "This is why dating sites are so dangerous," I've met nearly 100 men this way and he's the first that I've discovered has a history of scamming others.

His profile title is "Obama Senior Advisor Seeks Amazing Woman." Who wouldn't be drawn to that? Evidently, that's part of his scheme. We talked by phone a few times and set a time to meet.

At dinner he was intelligent, charming, and conversant in Obama's policies. He wasn't much to look at so he apparently depends on his words to attract people. He sprinkled the conversation with "You're beautiful," "I want to take you to Prague, the most romantic city in the world," "I want you to meet my son," and other signs of intended long-term interest. He even said, "I'd love to take you to the White House for lunch. Would you like to meet the president?"

Listening with a jaded ear not getting sucked in, I knew enough to need corroborating evidence before I believed this possible, but far-fetched story. There were inconsistencies — including how would this frumpily dressed man fit in with a world-class team? But I had no idea his stories were more than just a man trying to make a favorable first impression. It was the beginning of a grifter's wooing to extract funds from women.

I learned the truth by Googling him once I returned home, armed with his whole name — which I learned is an alias. I found several pages chocked full of complaints from both men and women stating he was a liar, manipulator, swindler, convicted fraud and scam artist, and has a practice of paying for business dealings by checks from closed accounts. He'd been fired from a number of jobs for fraud making stupid mistakes that made it easy to uncover his deception.

How do I know he's using an alias? The complaint page included his alias and disclosed his real name with a link to a social networking site where he posted the same picture as his online profile.

But it gets worse. He is also accused of grabbing female members of a social group in a predatory fashion, which caused him to be expelled, and of aggravated sexual harassment.

Here are some of his typical lies:

He's a cancer survivor (the cancer changes with the story)

Wife died of cancer 2 years ago

Is one of President Obama's 5 inauguration speech writers, and was on staff for 2 years in the campaign and is still on staff

Was on the faculty at several colleges in Chicago and Boulder

Was an executive for the largest PR firm in the country

Is courted by top politicians to write speeches and create strategy for them

Is a film and art columnist so gets tickets to opening nights

Is the author of a forthcoming book

How do you protect yourself from a smooth-talking sociopath? It's common sense that we sometimes don't heed when faced with a practiced scammer:

💚 Listen to uncommon stories with skepticism. Not that people can't accomplish amazing things, but verify from independent sources before believing them.

💚 Don't fall easily for early sweet talking. If you haven't heard it in a while, "You're beautiful," "I'm falling in like already," "I'd love to see you again" are alluring. However, if said too often too

early, they are signs that something is amiss as he
barely knows you.

💜 Guard your privacy, not giving much personal
information about where you live, if you own or
rent, or your financial situation.

💜 Google him using various pieces of information
he told you in case he's using an alias.

Will you be able to avoid all scammers? No. but
these tips will help you uncover some early. Try to balance healthy skepticism with being open. I know it's
hard, but there are people who have done amazing
things. But don't believe their stories until you've verified them from other sources.

Should you tell him he's crossed the line?

In the getting-to-know-you stage, you're wrong if you tell a man he's crossed the line and wrong if you don't.

If you do, you can be seen as controlling. If you don't, you give the impression that whatever he did/said is fine with you. Or you can just disappear and he'll never know why.

Last night, I was having an online chat (which I don't often do) with a guy who's flirted with me for a week or so via email. This was the first time we chatted real time, although I'd given him my phone number, but he didn't call. (That is a sign right there.)

After 15 minutes, this dean of a university tells me how "WELL ENDOWED" (his caps) he is. I told him that was nice, but too much info at this stage in getting to know each other. Since we'd been talking about keeping fit, and things related to physicality, I took it in that vein. After my TMI comment, he told me he was referring to his academic status.

Uh huh.

Later on, keeping in the academic theme, he offered that he wanted to study me to learn what I liked. He said he wanted to be ready for the "ORALS" (again, his all caps).

When I said I'd rather keep the conversation non-sexual at this point, he said I wanted to control the "pace" (whatever that means) of the conversation. I said I didn't want to go sexual with our first real-time discussion.

While I'm not a prude and can banter and whip out the double entendres and innuendos as quickly as a man, there is a time and place. The first conversation is not that time.

I've heard men advise women that we must have standards on what behaviors we'll accept. We must show men how we want to be treated and if they insist on not treating us with the regard we require, move on. I was attempting to do just that.

I've also had conversations with men where I didn't speak up. I just extricated myself as soon as possible. He never knew why I didn't respond to him after that. I debate rather to tell a man why we won't be going out, and have decided if he is really interested he'll ask. But for me to offer an explanation to an obtuse man is really just speaking to the wind as he'll never get it.

What's your policy on speaking up if a potential date crosses the line? Do you say something or just quietly drift away never to be heard from again?

Are you talking yourself out of potential dates?

I mean this literally — not are you internally talking yourself out of going on a date.

For example, recently I had two conversations with a new guy. About 30 minutes into the second conversation, I said I needed to get back to work. He asked if I'd like to get together. I said, "Sure, we could meet for coffee. What part of town do you live in?"

He responded that he lived near an upscale shopping center that I like to frequent.

"Great. We could meet there."

He then launched into a 10-minute rant about how he wasn't into expensive dinners, he rarely went to nice restaurants, etc., etc., etc., ad nauseam.

I had suggested coffee, not dinner, and the more he

talked and repeated himself, the less I wanted to meet him.

Finally, I repeated that I needed to go. He said he'd like to meet me but he would leave it to me to contact him if I wanted to get together. I politely said okay and hung up.

It was not only his assuming I was after an expensive dinner when I'd clearly stated coffee, but his repetition was irritating. Then there was the fact that I do like nice dinners once in a while and I knew I wouldn't really be happy with someone who was allergic to white tablecloths.

I'm sure I have talked myself out of dates as well. The challenge is we have no idea what we said that was off-putting to the other.

Some say email and phone filtering is effective as it reveals mis-matched characteristics quickly without going to the trouble of actually meeting. But part of me wonders if we aren't limiting our choices by judging someone on a sliver of information. On the other hand, these conversations often telegraph values and preferences enough that you know you are too different to be a match.

Have you been interested in someone until they talked too much? Have you felt someone's interest wane as you talked on the phone? Do you think weeding someone out over the phone is effective, or do you give them the benefit of the doubt and meet anyway?

Are your early contact expectations out of whack?

In the early getting-to-know you stage of dating, it's not unusual for there to be some miscommunication. However, how one handles these hiccups tells you a lot about the person's thinking. This is a good thing, as if their thinking is 180-degrees off from yours, you learn early that you aren't a match.

Today I received a call from a nice potential suitor, with whom I'd exchanged a few emails and had a good, lengthy first call last week. He is intelligent, a good conversationalist, articulate, and clear on what he's looking for. At the end of that first conversation, he said he liked our conversation very much and wanted to meet me in the next few weeks when he visits some clients in my area, a 2-hour drive from him.

I said that was a great idea. We agreed that if one of us had the itch to call the other in the interim, to feel free to dial the other's digits.

Clear, right? Transparent, right? We both thought so.

His call today was prompted by another women from the same site "chewing him out." After an initial conversation with her, he also left it that he'd call when he arranged his calendar to be in her area. In the second call, however, she chastised him for not calling sooner nor arranging to meet her immediately. He was taken aback.

He was concerned that he might not be meeting my expectations either and didn't want to blow it with me. I explained that I was fine with how we left it. Had he pressed for an immediate meeting, he might have appeared a bit desperate. I assured him that if he was as clear with her as he was with me, she was being needy, not him being neglectful.

He was concerned that he might not be meeting my expectations

After the initial shock when I've received calls similar to the one he received, I've been grateful that the man showed his true colors so early on. I consider it ducking a big bullet as we know how much time and emotional energy we can invest in someone who seems like they might be a good match for us. By seeing the mismatch early on it saved us a lot of energy.

I was impressed at this man's taking responsibility for ensuring he and I had the same understanding. I think it takes a strong person to broach what could be an awkward conversation.

When I was beginning to date, I now see how my neediness and loneliness could have prompted expectations like the woman who'd chewed out my new friend. I didn't know how relationships evolved and thought that if a man was interested in me, he should be pursuing me, damnit! And fast! And if we didn't quickly go to talking every day, I thought he was a player or just not that into me.

Now I realize that relationships take time to build. If a man starts calling me every day and we haven't even met — that's a red flag. Whenever that's happened, it's spelled trouble. And if I expect him to call every day and then chew him out for not doing so, something's wrong — and generally it's with my expectations.

Have you had someone chastise you for not meeting their expectations early in dating? If so, did you continue to see them or call it quits? Have you ever chewed out someone for not behaving like a sweetie when you're really just getting to know each other?

Granny panties, schoolmarm and Church Lady

It continually amazes me to hear the comments some men make during the pre-date stage. You would think they would focus on putting their best foot forward, thinking about how they want to make a great impression.

But no.

Some (many?) seem to have no filter or editor and just spew forth whatever is on their mind.

Case in point, the comments made in this posting's title. Let me explain.

I have a dozen pictures posted on a dating site. I like all of them (or I wouldn't have posted them) and they show me in a variety of settings from professional, formal, informal, to fun. I've received many, many compliments on my pics.

However, occasionally a man makes contact and we'll start chatting. Either these men quickly become comfortable with me or they have no aforementioned filter. Then they let some disparaging comment slip.

Does a man really expect me to react positively when he says I look like I'd wear granny panties? Or that I epitomize a schoolmarm? Or that a picture of me in a wide-brimmed straw hat (which I've been told numerous times is classy and fetching) looks like I'm the Church Lady?

After perusing all my pics, a man asked, "Which is the real you?" A ridiculous question I thought — they were all the real me. So I asked what he meant. He said, "You look like you put on some pounds since the previous pic," which I had not. It was the angle of the camera. While I could appreciate that many people post decades old and many-pounds-ago pics, I do not. I guess it was how he asked that was off-putting to me.

Do these men think at all before letting forth whatever crosses their mind?

On the one hand, honesty can be refreshing and appreciated. But honesty is generally valued most when you've built trust and have a solid relationship established. Honesty like "You look like you put on some pounds since the previous pic" is not appealing.

What have you had potential dates say to you that was off-putting? How did you handle it?

Feeling smothered

When someone likes another, the "liker" wants a lot of contact with the "likee." However, if the ardor isn't equal, the likee can feel smothered. Case in point: I'm getting to know a new guy, thus far only by phone. He calls several times a day. Recently, I called him back from an airport and he asked me to call him when I got home so he knew I'd arrived safely.

> *The likee can feel smothered.*

While I appreciate his concern for my safety, I haven't had to check in with someone about my safe arrival since I lived with my parents. So I didn't. He left two voice mails when he thought I'd gotten home. I returned them the next day, as this wasn't important to me and felt like a chore, not something I relished.

When one hasn't yet even met a person, I think one call a day is sufficient — and even that can be overkill. I've been drawn into extensive text and IM conversations with guys before I've met them and have learned it's usually a time sink. Yes, it can be fun and flirtatious, but if there's no chemistry when you meet, then it's all for naught.

The challenge is to assert one's needs for not-so-frequent contact without hurting the other. If I'm not yet comfortable saying it outright, then I wait to respond, rather than replying instantly. Although if the liker isn't astute enough to understand that too-frequent communication can be off-putting, he is not likely to get the subtlety of tardy responses.

When I am the stalker, er, I mean liker, and make too-frequent contact, I surmise that less-than-quick responses mean to lay off. I may be misinterpreting this as perhaps the person has been unable to respond. So if he responds enthusiastically, and with "I'm so bummed I couldn't respond immediately," that quells the doubts. But without that feedback, I look for the subtleties.

Video vetting

"I will only date a woman who video chats" my tech-savvy friend declared.

"What if she is like me, and doesn't video chat because no one looks good webcasting?"

"It would take a lot for me to want to start dating a woman who doesn't do video."

"Some of us are too vain!"

"Let me ask you this: would video chatting have prevented you from wasting a lot of time talking to men who, when you met them, looked nothing like their pictures?"

> *"Some of us are too vain!"*

"Of course. There are those who post only pictures from decades ago."

"And when you met them, didn't you wonder about their judgment to post decades-old pics, but not recent ones, thinking they still looked like that?"

"Absolutely!"

"Did any of those men who didn't match their pics ever make it beyond a coffee date?"

"No."

"There you have it!"

"However, I will also say I've eliminated men who one-way video chatted with me because they let their hair down, so to speak. Maybe I was being too picky."

"Or maybe you were saving yourself several hours of meeting someone who would go nowhere."

"But no one looks good on video chat! The lighting is bad, the angle is bad. I don't want to have to do my hair and makeup every time someone wants to video chat!"

"But look at the time it would save you from meeting up with men who aren't appealing!"

I guess my friend is right. But I'm still not keen on suggesting it. I've had men ask me if I'll video chat and I've always declined. Some of them have chatted one way, which is a little odd. It's not too bad if you've already met and have an idea of what they look like in person.

What do you think about video chatting before meeting? Good idea or bad?

Feeling like a mail-order bride

Y ou've struck up a nice communication with a man who seems to fit many of your criteria. He's smart, educated, polite, funny, well traveled, successful and clearly interested in you and your life. His age, height, and economics are in the right range for you. You've talked on the phone several times and you've had email, IM or text conversations every day for a week.

You usually like to meet a man in person within a week or 10 days — before spending too much time flirting virtually. You know it pretty much all hinges on how you feel about each other face-to-face. It can enhance your growing fondness toward each other, or it can fall flat.

With a first date set for a few days hence, for whatever reason (business or family illness) your guy is suddenly called out of town. You understand — he must go. But it happens too quickly to fit in even a coffee date to meet.

While he's gone, he calls daily, IMs and emails you sweet messages. The conversations focus around each other's needs and desires. You feel you're really getting to know each other — as much as one can without being in the same room. He expresses his deepening fondness towards you, how much he wishes he were with you, how he can't wait to meet you.

As you both share more and more, his expressions of endearment increase. He asks your favorite clothing designer and says he'd like to buy you some of that line. He asks where you would optimally like to live, then says he'll build you a house there. He asks where you'd like to travel, then says he'll take you there. On and on he continues to unearth your desires and tells you he'll provide them.

His expressions of endearment increase.

You know it is infatuation and idealization, based on words not actions. When he says he can't wait to have you share the same last name, it hits you: This must be how mail order brides feel! Men who want a woman to move across the country or world are wooed by sweet talk and promises from a man they've never met! Luckily, the man who's sweet talking you lives a few miles away and isn't intending to move to some remote part of the world — as far as you know.

But unlike many mail order brides, you know to

be skeptical. You know not to count on any promises made by someone you haven't met. Heck, you know not to count on promises made by some people you *have* met! You know that he is just flirting and trying to say things he thinks will please you. Yet you are clear these suggestions of promises are a sign of his neediness. But since there doesn't seem anything malicious, you give him grace. You are also on guard because you this is how scammers bilk lonely hearts out of their life's savings.

What was she thinking?

A 25-year-old woman agreed to meet — for the first time — a man she'd connected with through a dating site at his house at 9 p.m. to go out to dinner. When she arrived at his door, he grabbed her by the hair and pulled her inside. There, a gun-toting accomplice demanded her keys and the two men drove off in her car.

This is a tragic story.

But it is also a story of stupidity. She was 25 — old enough to know better. But she did not have enough sense to know it was stupid to meet a man for the first time at his house!

> *This is a tragic story.*

Yes, she is a victim.

But really, some people are victims because of their lack of good decision making.

What are the chances this could happen to you? I hope very low. Because you are older and, I trust, much wiser.

The reason this made the news is because it was an anomaly. But there are plenty of other tales of bad stuff that's happened to women on a date that they are too embarrassed to report.

This underscores why you should never make an exception to meeting a man in a public place the first few times.

Somethin' somethin' on the side

A recent conversation with a guy pal was startling.

He's a smart, goal-oriented, ethical, solid-morals, middle-class guy. So I assume he hangs out with other like-minded folks. But apparently not so much.

He shared that every one of his friends has "something on the side." Meaning whether married or in a relationship, all of them have either a go-to booty call provider or a regular mistress/lover on the side.

I was so dumfounded I didn't have the presence of mind to probe for more details. So I don't know if it is true for both men and women, married and those in relationship but not married, only true for long-time relationships, or what.

So we have to make some assumptions until I get more data. We have to assume that, based on his blanket comment, that this is true for both genders, across socio-economic strata for all races in his circle of friends.

Wow.

If his social circle is an indication of much of America, it is depressing. If so, politicians and celebrities aren't the only ones who take license with the concepts of commitment and fidelity. What is commonly believed to be an affliction of those with power has now filtered down to those with the inclination to cheat, no matter what their social status.

It is not news that people from all parts of society cheat. What was shocking to me is this man's observation that so many do so. He said all of his friends, not just a few.

People from all parts of society cheat

What are the implications for us midlife daters?

If we are constantly suspicious, it kills the relationship. But if we're naive, we can get taken advantage of, as well as possibly be inflicted with deadly diseases.

Does this mean that if you're becoming serious with someone you should hire an investigator? Some do. Seems a bit overkill unless you have some evidence.

Generally, I suggest people proceed slowly. It helps you note the person's modus operandi. If after a few weeks, you notice he only pays in cash, only wants to

come to your house, whenever you call in the evening, he says he has to call you back, these are some indications there's another woman involved.

In fact, I suggest you don't get serious until you've been to his house at least a few times. Get a little snoopy. Look in the bathroom cabinets. Are there lady products and he doesn't share the bath with a daughter? He may shrug them off as leftovers from his last sweetheart. But just notice quantities and if some have been used when you come back.

Am I encouraging you to automatically be suspicious? A little. I've been taken in by cheaters and in retrospect, I could have been more astute, thus protecting my heart and my health.

The key, I believe, is to be open but cautious. Don't accuse him of anything you don't have solid evidence of. But also don't believe lame explanations because you are smitten. Protect your heart.

Resources

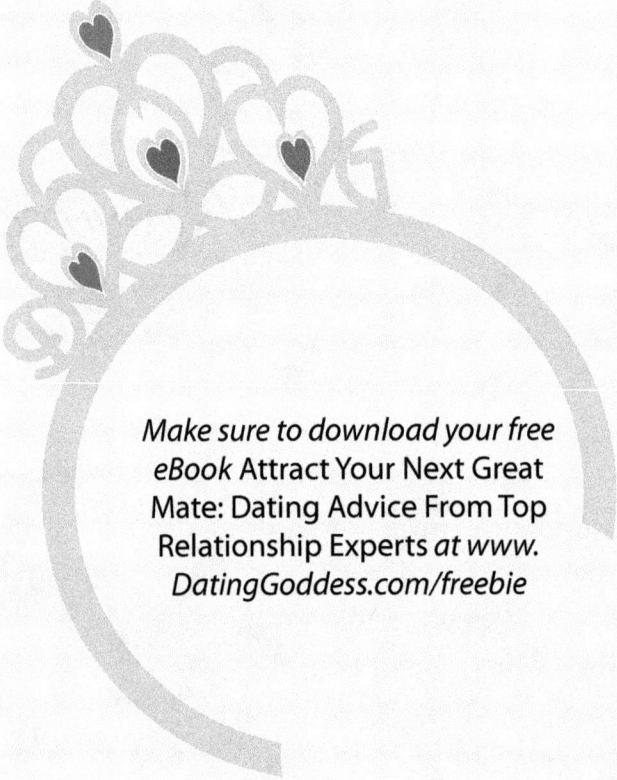

Make sure to download your free eBook Attract Your Next Great Mate: Dating Advice From Top Relationship Experts *at www. DatingGoddess.com/freebie*

Afterword

A t the time of this writing, I have not yet found my true King Charming. I continue my search with verve. I've become more discerning about what I want and don't want. I've met some wonderful men pals — my treasures — who continue to be in touch.

I wish you much luck in your adventure. It will be fun and frustrating, exhilarating and exasperating, and sexy or sexless. So much depends on you, your approach and your attitude. My books are designed to help you enjoy as much as possible and ward off unpleasantness. But nearly all adventures have wonderful highs as well as a few lows. If you know that going in and arm yourself with information on what to expect, you'll have more of the positives and fewer of the negatives.

Please drop by www.DatingGoddess.com and join in the discussion and report on your experiences.

Dating Goddess

R*esources*

Go to www.datinggoddess.com to access a variety of useful resources. We work to suggest resources we think have value.

Dating and relationship book reviews

These reviews will save you time and money as I've given you my take on specific books, CDs and more. Some are worth your effort to buy and read or listen to them — some are not. We're always adding new book reviews, so check frequently. We'll also notify our mailing list when new resources are added.

Dating site links

There are a lot of dating sites on the Internet. I've listed the ones I think are worth investigating.

Dating products and tools

Dating can be daunting. We're continually looking at

ways to make it easier and more fun. We'll provide info on games, tools, even date-wear that will help others know you're available, or help you get to know potential suitors better.

Dating and relationship advice sites

Advice "experts" abound on the Internet as anyone can self-proclaim themseves as expert — even if they haven't dated in 30 years and never in midlife. I've worked to find experts who's advice I generally think is solid.

Midlife recources

We'll feature Web sites, books, events and other resources we think might interest you.

Newly discovered resources

I'll add other resources as we discover them, subscribe to our mailing list to get the scoop as soon as we find them. Go to www.DatingGoddess.com to register for our mailing list. Don't worry, we won't sell or give your email to anyone.

Acknowledgments

Let me start by acknowledging the 112 men who helped trigger the lessons contained in this book. Some prompted several! They remain nameless here to protect their identity, although most would recognize references to them. Plus the thousands more whose winks, emails and calls didn't result in a date, but helped me learn the dating game. And all those men who I emailed who never responded — such a blessing to have them weed themselves out.

I acknowledge the 112 men who triggered my lessons

I'd like to thank my Seven Sisters mastermind group for the tremendous brainstorming, noodling, strategizing and encouragement. I wouldn't have begun this project without the prodding of Val Cade, Chris Clarke-Epstein, Mariah Burton Nelson, Sue Dyer, Sam Horn and Marilynn Mobley.

Thank you to my good friends who've listened to my dating stories ad nauseam, and whose support and wisdom are embedded in this text. Ed Betts, Ken Braly, Bruce Daley, Tom Drews, Elaine Floyd, Paulette Ensign, Scott Friedman, Craig Harrison, Mary Jansen, Tom Johnson, Sandy Jones, Mary Kilkenny, Ellie Klevins, Patrick Lynch, Mary Marcdante, Barbara McNichol, Ann Peterson, Anthony Ramsey, Caterina Rando, Kristy Rogers, Jana Stanfield, Holly Steil, Terry Tepliz, and George Walther, thank you.

The Adventures in Delicious Dating After 40 series

The *Adventures in Delicious Dating After 40* series is designed to help you understand your own midlife dating journey. It is not a road map, as we all take different routes. It is a guide to help you understand yourself, midlife men, and the dating process. Hopefully, you'll not only learn from the lessons and insights shared in this series, but you'll examine how they apply — or don't — to your own dating adventure.

You'll get the scoop on what you need to know, what's changed since you last dated, and how to navigate inevitable bumps in the road.

Following is an overview of each book in the series and a sampling of some of the chapter titles. All are detailed at www.DatingGoddess.com.

Date or Wait: Are You Ready for Mr. Great?

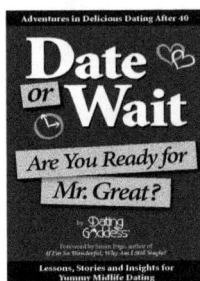

Are you ready for a special man in your life? You have a great life. But you know you'd like a special man to share it. You think you're ready to date, but you haven't done it in a while.

What should you consider before you actually start dating full bore? Even if you've reentered the dating world, this will give you a foundation of attitude and philosophy to make your adventure more fulfilling.

Sample chapters

💗 From hurt to flirt

💗 Dating is like Baskin-Robbins

💗 You've got to kiss a lot of…princes!

💗 What's your definition of dating success?

💗 Are you open to receiving?

💗 Dating: A self-designed personal-growth workshop

💗 Hands-on dating research

💗 Being present to the presents

💗 Being aggressively single

💗 Approaching dating like a buffet

💗 Is Brad Pitt ruining your love life?

💗 Treasures can come in dented packages

Assessing Your Assets: Why You're A Great Catch

You have many wonderful quali-
ties. But it's easy to focus on one's flaws
— at least what seem like flaws to you.
However, to the right man your imperfections are endearing, attractive
and lovable. You have to be clear what
you offer a man who will find you enchanting.

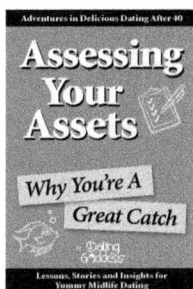

Assessing Your Assets helps you look at what you bring
to a new relationship. It will help you see your good points
so you'll approach dating with more confidence.

Sample chapters

💚 Don't think you are damaged goods

💚 You are (probably) more attractive than you think!

💚 They aren't called "hate handles"

💚 Are you a good man picker?

💚 What are your deal breakers?

💚 Are you arguing your limitations?

💚 Turn your liabilities into assets

💚 The strong vs. nice woman debate

💚 Is your sense of humor stunting your dating?

💚 Why are we drawn to bad boys?

💚 The zest test

In Search of King Charming: Who Do I Want to Share My Throne?

You are no longer looking for "Prince" Charming because you are a queen. You want someone who is at your level, not groveling at your feet. You want a king — someone who's your equal and with whom you can rule the throne together!

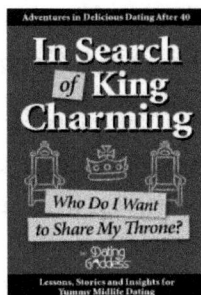

This book focuses on helping you better define what you want beyond tall, dark and handsome! You'll consider characteristics you might not have thought of before. You'll look at what you want now.

Sample chapters

💜 Building your Franken-boyfriend

💜 What's your "perfect boyfriend's" job description?

💜 A man to go with your wardrobe

💜 In search of the elusive good kisser

💜 When you're clear on what you want, it appears

💜 Are you dating the same guy in different bodies?

💜 Does he fit in your world?

💜 What's your kissing quotient?

💜 Is your guy's loving muscle strong?

💜 Do you both have the same dating rhythm?

Embracing Midlife Men:
Insights Into Curious Behaviors

Do you sometimes scratch your head after interacting with a midlife man, wondering, "What could he possibly be thinking?" Especially if it's before, during or after a date with a man who presumably wants to impress you!

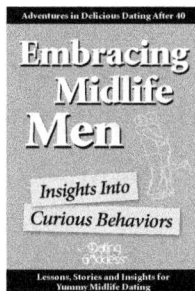

This book focuses on better understanding midlife men's behaviors. When you grasp what's going on in his head it's much easier to embrace him. Men are wondrous creatures, so we need to understand them better and love them for who they are.

Sample chapters

🖤 Men are like shoes

🖤 Why men disappear when it gets serious

🖤 Chivalry isn't dead —but it seems to be hibernating

🖤 Do men want feisty women?

🖤 Midlife men have forgotten how to date

🖤 Are you getting prime time from your man?

🖤 When a man tells you what he paid for things

🖤 Does he treat you like his ex?

🖤 Has Greg Behrendt done women a disservice?

🖤 Tales of woo

Dipping Your Toe in the Dating Pool: Dive In Without Belly Flopping

You've decided you are ready — you want to start dating. Maybe you've already had a few coffee dates with several men. You want to be as successful as possible on your dating adventure.

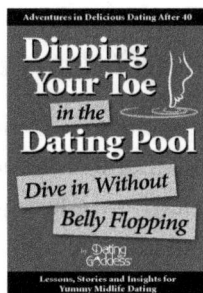

This book focuses on getting started on your dating adventures. We cover what you need to know as you begin your journey.

Sample chapters

💜 Do you have the right datewear?

💜 Dating with integrity

💜 Building your rejection muscle

💜 When "be yourself" is questionable advice

💜 Faux beaus and practice dating

💜 Are you making bad decisions out of loneliness?

💜 Being "in wonder" about your date's behavior

💜 When do you feel most vulnerable in dating?

💜 Are you out of his league — or he yours?

💜 Why listening is so seductive

Winning at the Online Dating Game: Stack the Deck in Your Favor

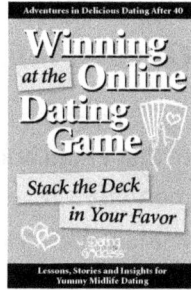

Internet dating can be frustrating or fruitful. It will be much less exasperating if you know how to read and weed out men's profiles that aren't appropriate for you. And you'll have a steady stream of potential suitors if you know how to write a compelling profile for yourself.

This book focuses on the ins and outs of online dating. How to play the game, which has it's own rules and language. If you don't understand how online dating works, you'll waste a lot of time connecting with men who are not a possible fit for you.

Sample chapters

💜 Shopping for men

💜 Safe online dating

💜 Is 21st Century dating unnatural?

💜 What do men look at in your profile?

💜 Euphemisms uncovered

💜 Are you describing yourself compellingly?

💜 No, I will not be dating your Harley

💜 Playing the online dating game

💜 Scantily clothed pictures

Check Him Out Before Going Out: Avoiding Dud Dates

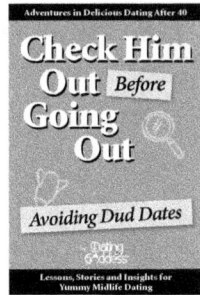

Under the cloak of the anonymity that email and the phone provides, men often reveal more than they intend. If you ask the right questions you can find out a lot about his values and view of the world after just an interaction or two.

This book focuses on what you need to ask before agreeing to even a coffee date. You need to vet the men who email and call you to ensure you're not likely to waste your time with men who clearly aren't a match.

Sample chapters

💚 Becoming smitten with the fantasy

💚 Can Google help — or hinder — your dating life?

💚 Qualify your potential dates before meeting

💚 The art of consideration

💚 Anticipating a big date is like awaiting Santa

💚 Being seduced by what he is over who he is

💚 Are you his spare?

💚 My boyfriend, whom I haven't met

💚 When canceling is the right thing to do

💚 Politics, religion and sex — oh my!

First-Rate First Dates: Increasing the Chances of a Second Date

You can tell a lot about someone within the first 30 minutes. What does he talk about? Does he ask you questions? If so, what does he want to know about you? What do you need to know about him? How does he treat you? How does he treat those around you?

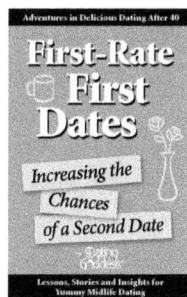

This book focuses on what goes on during the first date. How do you determine if you want a second date? What you can do to increase the likelihood your date will ask you for a second? That is if you want a repeat!

Sample chapters

💚 Start with coffee

💚 How do you greet him?

💚 When it clicks, throw out some of your criteria

💚 Tracking your date's score

💚 Clues a guy is just looking for a booty call

💚 12 signs he won't be asking for a second date

💚 First-date red flags that this guy isn't for you

💚 Honesty is not always the best policy

💚 Chemistry, or does he make my toes curl?

💚 Women's first-date blunders

Real Deal or Faux Beau: Should You Keep Seeing Him?

You've begun to go out with a man you like. How do you decide if you should continue seeing him, or if you should release him because he's not The One?

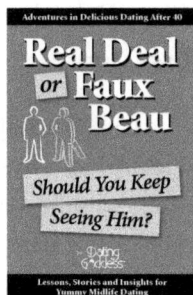

This book focuses on second dates and beyond. During the dating process you are both assessing if you want to keep seeing each other. This book helps you determine what questions you need to ask yourself.

Sample chapters

🖤 Deciding to see him again or not

🖤 What's your date's Delight/Disappointment Scale score?

🖤 Broaching tough conversations

🖤 "I want to respect me in the morning"

🖤 Does he invite you to his place?

🖤 Are you stingy in dating?

🖤 When his hand is on your knee too soon

🖤 Easy way to ask hard questions

🖤 Rose-colored glasses obscure red flags

🖤 If his stories don't add up, subtract yourself

Multidating Responsibly: Play the Field Without Being A Player

Playing the field is frowned on in some circles. There are definitely appropriate and inappropriate ways to date several men simultaneously.

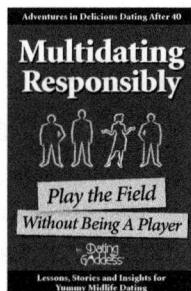

This book focuses on how to date around responsibly and with integrity without leading men on. If you do it with honesty, you can date several people at once until you're both ready to focus only on each other.

Sample chapters

💜 "Pimpin'" — Dating multiple guys

💜 Multi-dating pros and cons

💜 Your Date-A-Base — tracking multiple suitors

💜 "Hot bunking" your beaus

💜 Are you a "Let's Make a Deal" type of dater?

💜 Assume there are other women

💜 Dating's revolving door

💜 How long do you hedge your bet?

💜 Beware of multi-tasking when multi-dating

💜 Back burner beaus

💜 The boyfriend phone

Moving On Gracefully: Break Up Without Heartache

"Breaking up" sounds so high school, doesn't it? But part of the dating process is saying something when one of you decides not to date the other anymore. Going "poof" is not a mature or respectful option in midlife.

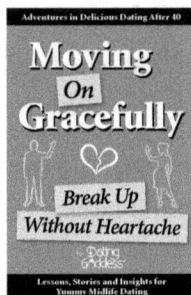

This book focuses on surviving a breakup, whether you initiate it or not. Either way, it's never easy to break up if you have developed any fondness toward the other.

Sample chapters

🖤 Hello — goodbye: How to say no thanks after meeting

🖤 Releasing back into the dating pool

🖤 50 ways to leave your lover? 4 ways not to leave your suitor

🖤 Breaking up is hard to do — right

🖤 Why men go "poof"

🖤 How to trump being dumped

🖤 When breaking up is a "Get Out of Jail Free" card

🖤 How to detect the end is near

🖤 Failed relationships' blessings

🖤 He's broken up with you — he just didn't tell you

🖤 Rejection is protection

From Fear to Frolic: Get Naked Without Getting Embarrassed

This book focuses on what you need to consider and know before getting physically intimate with a man you're dating. This is nerve-wracking to many midlife women. This book will prepare you.

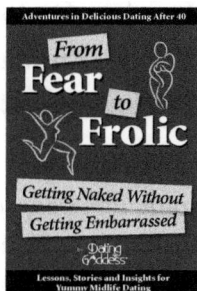

Sample chapters

💜 Sleepover do's and don'ts

💜 Does he want in your life — or just in your bedroom?

💜 Getting naked with him the first time

💜 An excuse to seduce or how important is bedroom bliss?

💜 What to ask yourself before getting naked with him

💜 Are you and your guy on the same sexual time line?

💜 Sharing your sexual owner's manual with him

💜 What women need from a man before having sex

💜 Why too-soon midlife sex is like non-fat food

💜 How dating sex is like waffles

💜 Too-soon seduction: "I'm special, but not THAT special"

Ironing Out Dating Wrinkles: Work Through Challenges Without Getting Steamed

Nearly all relationships have some ups and downs. Part of getting to know someone is knowing how they work through relationship misunderstandings.

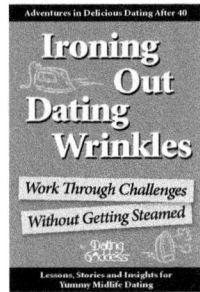

This book focuses on how to work through the inevitable hiccups that happen when you are getting to know each other. If you can both deal with challenges, the bond deepens and you find yourself smitten.

Sample chapters

❤ When your guy vexes you, ask what your highest self would do

❤ The first fight

❤ You want boo; he wants boo-ty

❤ Where's the line between getting your needs met and being selfish?

❤ Expressing your upset with your guy

❤ Is his toothbrush in your cabinet too soon?

❤ Do you love how he loves you?

❤ Is he collecting data on how to make you happy?

❤ Be careful of being smitten

❤ Exclusivity: How and when to broach it

www.ingramcontent.com/pod-product-compliance
Lightning Source LLC
Chambersburg PA
CBHW051737020426
42333CB00014B/1353